AF268777

JUST A CRAZY OLD WOMAN WRITES POETRY

Jacquelyne Bielinski

JUST A CRAZY OLD WOMAN WRITES POETRY

Copyright © 2019 # TXu 2-142-146 by The Jacquelyne N. Bielinski Trust dated December 24, 2003

All rights reserved. No part of this book may be used or reproduced in any manner whatsoever without written permission except in the case of reprints in the context of reviews.

ISBN: 978-1-7326507-0-1

Printed in the United States of America

THANK YOU

THANK YOU OF COURSE EACH KNOW WHO YOU ARE

THANK YOU YOUR LOVE HAS BROUGHT ME THIS FAR

THANK YOU FOR BELIEVING IN YOURSELF

THANK YOU FOR SHARING A LIFE FILLED WITH WEALTH

THANK YOU I WATCHED YOU BECOME YOUR BEST

THANK YOU YOUR CHARACTER IS WELL EXPRESSED

THANK YOU FOR MAKING ME FEEL THAT I MATTERED

THANK YOU THE STRENGTH WHEN ALL MY LIFE SHATTERED

THANK YOU WISH I COULD HAVE DONE SO MUCH MORE

THANK YOU FOR GRAND BABIES I TRULY ADORE

THANK YOU HARDLY DESCRIBES HOW I FEEL

THANK YOU I WISH IT HAD BEEN MORE IDEAL

THANK YOU NOT JUST BECAUSE I NEED TO

THANK YOU INSTEAD FOR YOU GIVING YOU

THANK YOU ARE WORDS THAT SAY LIKE IT IS

THANK YOU THAT WE'VE BEEN TOGETHER LIKE THIS

THANK YOU FOR BEING PART OF EACH OTHER

THANK YOU THE PRIVILEGE OF BEING YOUR MOTHER

THANK YOU IT'S BEEN LIKE A DREAM TO RECALL

THANK YOU FOR MAKING ME PROUD OF YOU ALL

Jackie B.

Contents

"JUST A CRAZY OLD WOMAN WRITES POEMS TO HERSELF

HER LIFE IN RHYME GATHERS DUST ON THE SHELF

IT'S NOT WITH A TALENT TO MAKE AN IMPRESSION

BUT RATHER HER VOICE TO GIVE IT EXPRESSION

FROM MEMORIES TO WORDS OPEN AND LOOK

AT A CRAZY OLD WOMAN STILL WRITING HER BOOK"

THAT'S WHY IT'S CALLED LIFE...

"TRUST BE THE KEEPER OF ALL THAT YOU HEAR

PROTECTING THE WAGES OF SIN

SURRENDER TO YOU ON A WING AND A PRAYER

ALL CONFESSIONS I HOLD WITHIN"

THOUGHTS

THOUGHTS WANDER PATHS THAT LEAD TO CREATE

DECISION QUESTION REASON DEBATE

THOUGHTS APPEAR FLUID CONFUSED OR CONTRIVED

RANDOMLY BRILLIANT OR UNORGANIZED

THOUGHTS PROCESS FEELINGS PASSION AND HURT

HELD SOMEWHERE DEEPLY OR SHARED IF YOU WOULD

THOUGHTS LINGERING WITH HAUNTING UNREST

REPEATING RETURNING STILL UNEXPRESSED

THOUGHTS WELCOME QUIET PAUSE ANALYZE

WRAPPED IN THE TRUTH OR COATED WITH LIES

THOUGHTS PLAY EMOTIONS IN MATTERS OF HEART

KEEP IT TOGETHER OR TEAR IT APART

3

THOUGHTS OVERLOAD BLURRING THE LINES

TANGLED AND TWISTED IN LIMITED TIME

THOUGHTS WARNING STOP BEGGING PERMISSION

NEW THOUGHTS REFRESHED IN BETTER CONDITION

WHY

THINK BACK TO THAT DAY AS I RECALL

I SAT ON THE PORCH ALONE SO SMALL

WITH SUN SHINING BRIGHTLY FELT SO COLD

WAITING FOR YOU BUT YOU ONLY PHONED

SHE CAME OUT TO TELL ME THE TERRIBLE NEWS

NEVER FOUND OUT THE EXCUSES YOU USED

SHE TOLD ME YOU WEREN'T COMING THAT DAY

AND CLOSED THE FRONT DOOR AS SHE WALKED AWAY

LEAVING ME TEARFUL STILL HOPING TO SEE

YOUR OPEN ARMS AS YOU RUN TOWARD ME

MY LIFE WAS IN TURMOIL CONSTANT HEARTACHE

LONGING FOR YOU AND HATING THE WAIT

I KNEW I DIDN'T BELONG IN THIS PLACE

WITH OTHER CHILDREN FILLING THE SPACE

QUIETLY WAITING AND AT TEACHER'S COMMAND

THE PENCIL BE MOVED FROM MY LEFT TO RIGHT HAND

QUESTIONING WHY I WANTED TO SHOUT

NEEDING TO KNOW WHAT THIS WAS ABOUT

THE ANSWER KEPT HIDDEN AND EVEN NOW

YOU ARE GONE AND I'LL NEVER KNOW HOW

IT HAPPENED AND STILL WISH I COULD HEAR

WHY DID YOU LEAVE ME THOSE PRECIOUS YEARS

JUST A CRAZY OLD WOMAN

JUST A CRAZY OLD WOMAN PONDERING LIFE

RAISED SEVEN CHILDREN AND TWICE A WIFE

WITH MEMORY FADING CAN HARDLY RECALL

THE WHIRLWIND OF TIME AND THEN ABOVE ALL

EVEN FLASHES OF PAST ARE FORGETFUL DREAMS

NOT MUCH IN THE FUTURE FOR POSITIVITY

JUST A CRAZY OLD WOMAN STILL HAPPY TO LAUGH

WAITING FOR ACHES AND PAINS TO PASS

ONCE A FAIR BEAUTY NEVER TOO WISE

ARMED WITH STRENGTH AND STILL SOME SURPRISE

IF EVER THERE WAS A REASON TO CHEER

FOR HER IT WOULD BE MISTAKEN DEAR

JUST A CRAZY OLD WOMAN IT'S HARD TO BELIEVE

THOSE AMBITIOUS DREAMS AND ATTEMPTS TO ACHIEVE

TO TAKE ALL THE WRONGS AND TURN THEM TO RIGHT

AND COME TO THE END WITHOUT LOSING THE FIGHT

THINKING THERE MIGHT BE JUST ONE THING LEFT

OF A LEGACY TO LEAVE AS A GIFT

JUST A CRAZY OLD WOMAN REACHED HER PLATEAU

CAN'T COPE WITH THE HEAT OR WINTER'S COLD SNOW

REMAINING CLEAR HEADED WHATEVER FOR

LOATHING THE MUNDANE AND NEEDING MUCH MORE

IN A MANNER OF SPEAKING AND WISHING SHE COULD

REASSEMBLE THE PAST TO EXTRACT THE GOOD

JUST A CRAZY OLD WOMAN TRYING TO FIGURE

WHAT'S BECOME OF THE IMAGE LOST IN THE MIRROR

CURLY HAIR GONE WITH THAT HINT OF RED

CROPPED CLOSE IN WHITE THROUGHOUT HER HEAD

STILL ADMIRABLE OF POSTURE AND HEIGHT

NOW WISTFULLY VOID OF YOUTHS VIBRANT LIGHT

JUST A CRAZY OLD WOMAN WRITES POEMS TO HERSELF

HER LIFE IN RHYME GATHERS DUST ON THE SHELF

IT'S NOT WITH A TALENT TO MAKE AN IMPRESSION

BUT RATHER HER VOICE TO GIVE IT EXPRESSION

FROM MEMORIES TO WORDS OPEN AND LOOK

AT A CRAZY OLD WOMAN STILL WRITING HER BOOK

SOLITUDE

WITH LOST COMPOSURE AND CHAOS RESUMED

BLINDING PAIN IN AN INSTANT REOPEN THE WOUND

MISTAKES LINK ANOTHER BUILDING THE CHAIN

THAT WEAKENS THEN BREAKS ONCE THEN AGAIN

TIME PLAYS THE ENEMY LEAVING NO ROOM

TO RECAPTURE FULFILLMENT VANISHED TOO SOON

UNPLANNED ACTION TURNED BAD DECISION

APPARENT MISTAKES WITH NO RECISION

DRAWING A BLANK NO SEMBLANCE OF ORDER

OVERWHELMING CYCLE OF EMOTIONAL TORTURE

WITHSTANDING EXHAUSTION FROM WITHERING SCHEMES

STILL REACHING KEEP SEARCHING IN FARAWAY DREAMS

DEFTLY MASTERED THE ART OF AGGRESSION

CONSIDERED IT A SOUGHT AFTER POSSESSION

CLEARLY THE NEED TO PROVE ONCE AGAIN

ULTIMATE POWER COMES FROM WITHIN

EMPTINESS BLOOMS IN THE LIFE OF THE WRITER

IN SOLITUDE ODDLY COMFORT GROWS WIDER

THE MAGIC

BRING ME THE MAGIC I DESPERATELY SEEK

FROM ANYONE LICENSED TO GIVE

FOR SELFISH REASONS I KNOW I SPEAK

OF FOR AS LONG AS WE BOTH SHALL LIVE

METHODICALLY USED IN PAST INDISCRETIONS

BY THOSE UNWORTHY AND TAINTED

APPARENTLY SECRETIVE PLEASE DON'T MENTION

MY NAME TO ONE WHO IS JADED

MAKE IT A POWERFUL POTION UNMEASURED

DISTRACTION TO HEIGHTEN THE SENSES

RELINQUISH THE POWER GIVE INTO THE PLEASURE

UNTIL THE SURPRISES HAVE ENDED

CREATED BY FALSE AND PRETENTIOUS CADS

FOR THE SOLE PURPOSE OF BARTER

UNABASHED I FEEL MYSELF GOING MAD

OR BECOMING THE TYPICAL MARTYR

WITH CHANGE OF HEART NO FATAL MISTAKE

TO BE USED FOR A THRILL OF THE MOMENT

IS ACTUALLY NOT THE MAGIC I SEEK

BUT RATHER THE FULL ATONEMENT

COMPENSATION FOR DAMAGES WELL RECEIVED

AND LACK OF APOLOGY NOTED

BUILT UP ANIMOSITY UNRELIEVED

NOW DETONATE IT'S EXPLODED

MEMORY

THE PEN THE PAPER THE MEMORY TO TRACE

THE UNMISTAKABLE LINES THAT SHAPE YOUR FACE

A DREAM TURNED REALITY FOR JUST A SHORT TIME

APPARENTLY JUST AN ILLUSION OF MINE

BELITTLE BERATE AND MAXIMIZE SCORN

HOW QUICKLY CAN JOY DIMINISH TO MOURN

LOVE THAT IS LOST LIKELY WELL DISGUISED

BY PRETENTIOUS OUTPOUR OF DELIBERATE LIES

ARTISTICALLY FILTER YOUR WIELDED DECEPTION

ALL FOR ACCEPTANCE OF STRANGERS RECEPTION

MARRED BY YOUR VANITY EASY TO THRILL

ARROGANT TO THE END DID YOU THINK IT A SKILL

14

TIME TURNS THE PEN AND THE PAPER TO ASH

THE MEMORY GONE NO RECALLING THE FLASH

OF A DREAM TURNED FIASCO SO FAR AWAY

IMPERVIOUS PAIN ON THIS BEAUTIFUL DAY

PAIN

PAIN IS THE NAME DIGGING IN WAY TOO DEEP

AND TAKES UP MY PERSONAL SPACE

WITH DAGGER IN HAND MAKES AN AWFUL SWEEP

INFLICTING THAT WHICH I CAN'T EMBRACE

I CATCH AND HURDLE IT A DISTANCE AWAY

SO FAR IT CAN NEVER RETURN

AND BURY THAT FIEND WITHOUT REGRET

NOT A SOUL NO ONE WILL MOURN

ALTHOUGH DAYS ARE DARK WITH LITTLE RELIEF

ALL CONSUMING IN MY DESPAIR

I AM THE STRENGTH AND THROUGH MY BELIEF

THAT CURSED PAIN HAD BETTER BEWARE

16

NEXT WEEK IS COMING AND YES IT WILL

TURN THE DARK INTO LIGHT ONCE AGAIN

SMILING I PLAN TO SAY AND FULFILL

FORGET YOU PAIN YOU LOSE I WIN

JUST A CRAZY OLD WOMAN WRITES POETRY

CONFESSION

CONFESSION MY MOTHER MY VOICE TO YOUR EARS

FOR ALL BE REVEALED AND THEN

THE SUM OF EXPRESSING WOULD TAKE SOME YEARS

OF ABSOLUTE TRUTHS BOUGHT AND SPENT

CAPTIVATING DRAMA YET TO UNFOLD

NOT GUILTY NO REMORSE TO FEEL

RELIEVING MY SUBCONSCIOUS GROWS COLD

INDICATIONS OF NOTHING TO HEAL

CONFESSION MY MOTHER OF MATTERS CLOSED

TO PAY FOR BREACH OF CONTRACT

GIVEN THE PUNISHMENT SELF-IMPOSED

WHILE DEFINING FICTION FROM FACT

DIVULGE INFORMATION STILL LOCKED INSIDE

COULD OPEN AN AGE OLD CHAPTER

OF ABUNDANT SECRETS HELD TOO TIGHT

PERHAPS HATRED OR BEAUTIFUL RAPTURE

CONFESSION MY MOTHER AS A FINE ART

TO EXTRACT THE PERSONAL SILENCE

OF PRIVACY HELD AND YET TO IMPART

FROM THOSE STILL LOOKING FOR GUIDANCE

TRUST BE THE KEEPER OF ALL THAT YOU HEAR

PROTECTING THE WAGES OF SIN

SURRENDER TO YOU ON A WING AND A PRAYER

ALL CONFESSIONS I HOLD WITHIN

THE JOKE

ONE OF MY MOTHER'S FAVORITE JOKES

AND THE ONLY ONE I RECALL

IS FUNNY IN A TYPICALLY JEWISH WAY

BUT EASILY RELATED TO ALL

WHEN THE TELEPHONE RINGS

A YOUNG WOMAN SAYS HELLO

GOOD MORNING DAUGHTER I HOPE YOU ARE WELL

I REALLY HAVE MISSED YOU SO

WHAT ARE YOU DOING AND IS THERE

A PLAN FOR YOUR DAY

OH MAMA WHAT A MESS I'M IN

AND CAN'T SEEM TO FIND MY WAY

I HAVE A MIGRAINE THE HOUSE IS DIRTY

THE HADASSAH IS COMING FOR LUNCH

MY HAIR IS A MESS THE KIDS ARE SCREAMING

I'M TEARFULLY IN A REAL CRUNCH

JUST A CRAZY OLD WOMAN WRITES POETRY

DEAR DAUGHTER DON'T WORRY JUST TRY TO RELAX

I HAVE THE PERFECT PLAN

I'LL HOP ON THE SUBWAY TAKE A QUICK BUS

AND GET THERE AS SOON AS I CAN

TAKE A FEW ASPIRIN AND DRESS YOURSELF

I'LL TAKE CARE OF THE MEAL

I'LL CLEAN UP THE HOUSE LOOK AFTER THE KIDS

 IT'S MY PLEASURE AND NOT A BIG DEAL

OH MAMA WHAT A HELP THAT WOULD BE

WITHOUT YOU IT WOULDN'T GET DONE

HOW HAPPY I AM THAT YOU CALLED JUST TODAY

I AM THE LUCKIEST ONE

SO MY DARLING HOW IS MY IZZY

YOU KNOW HE'S MY FAVORITE BOY

I KNEW HE WOULD MAKE A WONDERFUL HUSBAND

AND BRING YOU PLENTY OF JOY

21

IZZY THE YOUNG WOMAN REPEATED

AND BOTH WOULD QUIETLY WAIT

FOR EACH OTHER TO SPEAK AND SUDDENLY REALIZE

THIS PHONE CALL WAS A MISTAKE

SO YOU'RE NOT MARRIED TO MY IZZY

WELL PLEASE JUST SAY SOMETHING

DEAD SILENCE FOLLOWED WITH ONE LAST ANSWER

DOES THAT MEAN YOU'RE NOT COMING

FREE BIRD

NO ESCAPING THE FATE OF TIME'S PAST PLIGHT

RESPONSIBILITY HOVERS

REACHING THE IMPASSE DARK AS NIGHT

WHAT BURDEN IT UNCOVERS

TAKE FLIGHT AT LAST FROM WORRISOME TROUBLE

SPONTANEOUS PATH TO THE SKY

DAYS TURN TO YEARS LIFE IN A BUBBLE

I AM A FREE BIRD WITH VISION TO FLY

COLD TRUTH IS BLINDING SNOW IN THE WINTER

BRIGHT BUT PAINFULLY SORDID

NURTURED FOREBEARANCE TASTE OF BITTER

CLING TO WHAT JOYS ARE AFFORDED

CLOSING EYES FOR A DAYDREAM ESCAPE

GLEAN PATIENCE FOR WHAT'S ON THE HIGH

BREAKING THE MOLD TAKING NEW SHAPE

I AM A FREE BIRD YEARNING TO FLY

SEEK VALIDATION OF WORLDLY WONDER

NONCHALANT CALM IN A BREEZE

RELEASING THE LAYERS PULLING ME UNDER

LIBERATION AT LAST WITH EASE

GRAVITY LIFTED EMBRACING THE DARE

TO BECOME MYSELF SATISFY

THE NEED FOR ASSURANCE TO TAKE ME WHERE

I AM A FREE BIRD AND FINALLY FLY

THE ANGEL

SHE IS THE STRENGTH IN THE FACE OF ADVERSITY

A REMINDER OF HOW IT IS DONE

APPLAUSE FOR THE BALANCE SHE CARRIES SO PERFECTLY

AND NEVER BACKS AWAY FROM

THE BOILING POINT OF HIGHEST ANXIETY

ADDING FUEL TO THE FIRE

EMBRACING PAIN AND LOVE ITS ENTIRETY

INCREDIBLE FORCE TO ADMIRE

UNENDING EXHAUSTION TO FURTHER THE CAUSE

WITH WONDROUS SKILL TO MANAGE

SUMMONING BRAVE AND BEYOND ANY PAUSE

INTOLERABLE DISADVANTAGE

25

LOCKED IN THE POWER DETERMINATION

TO WEILD THE SABER OF LIGHT

MASQUERADE FEAR TO THE ONE OF CREATION

ILLUMINATING ANGEL OF MIGHT

THE WIN

THE PLAYERS ARE READIED SET ON THEIR MARKS

POISED TO PARTAKE OF THE GAME

WHO'S BETTER WHO'S FASTER CHASING THE HEART

WITH EACH TARGET POSITIONED TO CLAIM

IT'S RIGHTFUL PLACE AMONG PAST RECIPIENTS

NOW FOCUSED RACE TO THE END

THE ODDS OF AWARD WINNING ACHIEVEMENT

STRENGTHENED BY PERSERVERENCE

WILL THE ULTIMATE WINNER TAKE ALL OR

HESITATE UPON WHAT IT SEEMS

THAT RACING THROUGH OPEN DOORS

FROM THE PAST OF DISTANT DREAMS

IS A REALITY CHECK JUST TO ENSURE

THAT THE GOAL OF WHICH THEY OBSESS

COULD BE A DANGER ZONE NO MORE

THAN A TROPHY PRIZE TO POSSESS

ENGAGED IN THE MOMENT'S PERFORMANCE

PULSES WILD FOR THE THRILL

ROARING THE CHEERS OF IMPORTANCE

DO RAISE AND BOLSTER THE WILL

WITHOUT HESITATION SAFE TO SAY

WHATEVER THE OUTCOME IT'S CLEAR

THE WIN IS THE LOSS ON THIS FINE DAY

AS THE PLAYERS DISAPPEAR

I AM

I AM THE DESIGNER WHO SKETCHED THE WAY

CREATED MY LIFE'S JOY AND MISERY

I AM THE CONDUCTOR WITH BATON IN HAND

THE PAINTER'S PALETTE THE ARCHITECT'S PLAN

I AM THE IMPULSIVE THAT MAKES FOR HEADSTRONG

THE DECISION FOR CHOICES MADE RIGHT OR WRONG

I AM THE GUILT OF MY OWN ADMISSIONS

BUT SADLY IN PAST THERE ARE NO REVISIONS

I AM THE MOMENTUM TO INFLUENCE TIME

ON TRACK WITH PRESENT AND FUTURE COMBINED

I AM THE PESSIMIST SEEKING TO EASE

THE ELUSIVE BALANCE OF INNER PEACE

29

I AM THE CAUSE WITH NO ONE AT FAULT

SECURING THE SECRETS KEPT SAFE IN MY VAULT

I AM THE ONE WHO ATTEMPTS TO SURVIVE

BUT WHO IS THE ONE THAT KEEPS ME ALIVE

EMBRACE

EMBRACING THE MOMENTS THAT MAKE UP LIFE

DEMANDS DISAPPOINTMENTS REWARDS

LAUGHTER FOR HAPPINESS TEARS FOR STRIFE

THE BALANCE TO STRIKE THE CORD

CONSIDER ALL ASPECTS TOGETHER

COURAGE AND PURPOSE COMBINED

HARD TO IMAGINE HOW TO MEASURE

THE TENSION OF THE VERY FINE LINE

WITHSTANDING THIS LIFELONG PRESSURE

THE MOLD WE'RE EXPECTED TO FIT

NOT QUITE ABLE TO MEASURE

UP TO THE STANDARDS THEY SET

STILL SEEKING THE DREAM OF IDENTITY

IS NOT LIKE TIMING A RACE

UNTIL IT BECOMES A REALITY

SOMETHING SUBSTANTIAL TO EMBRACE

TODAY TOMORROW AND ALWAYS

A FROZEN SMILE ON MY FACE

THEIR GLANCES WITHOUT KNOWING

HOW STRUGGLING THROUGH THE DAILY PACE

RESULTS IN THOUGHTS IMPLODING

AS SIGNIFICANT TIME TURNS LAME

ABSOLUTE SILENCE SURROUNDS

MORNING TO NIGHT ALL THE SAME

WHILE LONLINESS CONFOUNDS

SELF NEGLECT WITH NO EXCUSE

A SORROWFUL SIGHT TO SEE

WITH ADVERSITY PRODUCED

OBLIVION TURNING ME

DOWNWARD INTO MY DEPRESSION

UNBALANCED IN A DAZE

LEAVING ME ABUNDANT QUESTIONS

IN THE UNCLEAR HAZE

GRASPING FOR RECHARGED SALVATION

LIKE REACHING FOR THE SKY

JUST ONE SIDED CONVERSATION

UPLIFTING DREAMS GONE BY

DISHEARTENED WITH NO RELIEF

WHILE TRACES OF BRIGHTER DAYS

LEAVE ME STILL IN DISBELIEF

TODAY TOMORROW AND ALWAYS

CLARITY

RANDOM THOUGHTS PLACED IN PROCESSION

THE POET'S ARTISTIC CURATOR

WIELDING WORDS MAKE AN IMPRESSION

DOES THAT MAKE ME A WORTHY CREATOR

OPEN MY MIND TO EXPRESS THE ATTRACTION

IT OCCURS TO ME THAT I MIGHT

THINK SOMEHOW IT WILL BRING SATISFACTION

AND CLARITY IN THE PAGES I WRITE

CONVINCED THESE STORIES IN RHYME

UNDERSTOOD BEST IN THE END

STAGING IS CLEAR AND CONCISE

RECOLLECTION OF TIME AS IT'S SPENT

CAPTURING FRAGMENTS OF PAST IS A RISK

BLURRING THE LINES OF CLARITY

OMITTING PARTS LIKE SPACE ON A DISC

OR FINE TUNING THE VIEW OF REALITY

IT'S A LOVE/HATE THING...

"A LIAR A THIEF AND A CHEAT AND MORE

A PERFECT DISASTER DOWN TO YOUR CORE

I LOVED YOU I HATE YOU WITH NO IN-BETWEEN

LIKE A TOXIC OLD HABIT NOW FINALLY CLEAN"

THE MUSIC

CAUGHT IN THE LIGHT I COULD BARELY SEE

MAKING HIS WAY CLOSER TOWARD ME

HE WAS TOO SHORT HIS HAIR TOO LONG

BUT HE HAD A STYLE AND JUST LIKE A SONG

THE MUSIC SET MY HEARTBEAT ON HIGH

WITH AN ATTRACTION I COULDN'T DENY

THERE WAS AN EASE WITH WHICH HE POSSESSED

MAGIC SURRENDER MY LOVE WITH LESS

THAN A SECOND THOUGHT OR A PRAYER

FOR WHAT MIGHT EVENTUALLY IMPAIR

THE BEST OF MY JUDGEMENT AT ANY COST

FACING THE MUSIC ALL MY WILL LOST

37

HE TEASED WITH A SMILE BOWED FOR THE DANCE

INTOXICATING SCENT THAT LEADS TO ROMANCE

DRAWING ME CLOSER NO SIGN OF CLASHING

RETURNING THE HOLD ALL MY THOUGHTS CRASHING

DOWN IN A SPIRAL SPINNING OUT OF CONTROL

LET THE MUSIC BEGIN LET A STORY UNFOLD

TOXIC

TAKEN ABACK YOU KISSED MY HAND

IT TOOK ME SOME YEARS TO UNDERSTAND

THOUGHT IT WAS YOUR OLD-WORLD STYLE

THEN REALIZED IT WAS HOW YOU PROFILE

VICTIMS YOU SO CAREFULLY CHOOSE

TO INFLICT YOUR WILY USE AND ABUSE

YOU CREATED SUCH A WELL-HIDDEN TALENT

COVERED YOUR SHORTFALLS AND APPEARED GALLANT

NO CODE OF HONOR EVEN LESS TRUST

GO STRAIGHT FOR THE HEART THAT WAS A MUST

THE COUNTLESS FACES A SEA OF NO NAMES

YOU DESTROYED WITH A SMILE FELT NO SHAME

A LIAR A THIEF AND A CHEAT AND MORE

A PERFECT DISASTER DOWN TO YOUR CORE

I LOVED YOU I HATE YOU WITH NO IN-BETWEEN

LIKE A TOXIC OLD HABIT NOW FINALLY CLEAN

IMPRESS ME

IMPRESS ME WITH SOMETHING I DON'T YET KNOW

A CHANGE FROM THE TURBULENT ROMEO

DO YOU HAVE A MEASURE OF SUBSTANCE

WITHOUT HESITATION OR RELUCTANCE

PROFOUNDLY MORE THAN JUST WHAT I SEE

IMPRESS ME WITH SOMETHING ELSE YOU COULD BE

IMPRESS ME WITH ONE WISH YOU COULD GRANT

WITH A MINIMAL EFFORT I KNOW THAT YOU CAN'T

CHANGE THE AGENDA YOU ALREADY MADE

FOR YOURSELF YOUR ACTIONS ARE SO WELL PLAYED

TRY TO DISPOSE OF THE ANGER I FEEL

IMPRESS ME WITH ONE LAST WISH SO I HEAL

IMPRESS ME WITH MORE THAN YOUR CONFIDENT SMILE

NEED SOME COMPASSION FOR AWHILE

A HINT OF CHARACTER IF YOU COULD SPARE

A DEEPER VERSION OF YOU TO SHARE

FLASHBACKS OF YOU ARE ALL THAT I'VE GOT

IMPRESS ME I DARE YOU TO FLASH WHAT YOU'RE NOT

YOU WILL

YOU WILL THINK OF ME SOMEDAY

AND WONDER WHERE I'VE GONE

AND PERHAPS IN SOME IRONIC WAY

FEEL REMORSE FOR WHAT YOU'VE DONE

MISS ME THEN WITHOUT A SOUND

MY LAUGH MY FACE MY EVERYTHING

NO CONNECTION TO TURN IT AROUND

BARELY AN OUTLINE YOU MUST HAVE SEEN

YOU WILL FIND YOU'RE THE LOSER

AND BROUGHT OUT YOUR WORST

BY THEN I'LL HAVE ANOTHER

WHO'S NOT LOOKING TO HURT

OR PLAY MY EMOTIONS

WITH INTENTIONAL BLAST

42

TRADE CALM FOR COMMOTION

LEAVE DISDAIN IN THE PAST

YOU WILL POSSESS NO REGRET

RESPONSIBILITY OR BLAME

WHEELS IN MOTION ARE SET

WHERE I CAN RECLAIM

THE FREEDOM TO LOVE

NO NEED TO MANEUVER

AND FIND I'M ENOUGH

GIVE WITHOUT TAKING COVER

43

YOU WILL NOT HAVE REASON

TO EXERCISE POWER

I'M FREE FROM THAT PRISON

SCHEMES DEVISED BY A LIAR

NIGHTMARES OF YOU STEADILY DIE

HAVING THE STRENGTH TO MOVE ON

AND KNOWING FOR CERTAIN THAT MY LIFE IS MINE

WITH PLEASURE OF KNOWING YOU WILL BE GONE

PAYBACK

YOU LEFT ME WITH A DEBT OF LOVE

I FOUND IN AN EMPTY ACCOUNT

PAYBACK PLUS INTEREST IS NOT ENOUGH

NO DEDUCTIONS IT'S THE FULL AMOUNT

MY MIND MANUEVERS OVER THE TRACK

OF DECEIPT YOU CAREFULLY PLANNED

HOW TO GIVE THE ULTIMATE PAYBACK

YOU SO WELL DESERVE IN THE END

SORRY NO CREDIT OFFERED IN LIEU

OF THE PAYBACK I'LL GLADLY PROVIDE

HONOR THE BALANCE OWED AND DUE

MATCHING SAME VALUE SUPPLIED

45

TIMING IS PERFECT POISED TO OUTSMART

WITH THE ULTIMATE PAYBACK DEFINED

THE EMPTY BOX YOU CALL YOUR HEART

LOVE AND KISSES I'M SMILING GOOD BYE

WHAT TOOK YOU SO LONG

TIME MOVED SLOWLY WHILE DRAWING US CLOSER

THOUGHT IN THIS LIFE SOMEHOW IT WAS OVER

BUT AND HOWEVER AND ALL THINGS ASIDE

I WAITED YOU WAITED AND FINALLY ARRIVED

UNEXPECTED AND NEW BURNING DESIRE

QUICKLY BUILDING FROM SPARKS TO THE FIRE

COMPELLING AND MUCH TO MY SURPRISE

GAVE MYSELF FREELY WITHOUT COMPROMISE

WHERE HAVE YOU BEEN ALL THE WHILE

MY LIFE IN YOUR HANDS A GIFT WITH A SMILE

ALWAYS HOPING NOT KNOWING OF ANY CONDITION

YOU'D COME ALONG NOW REACHING FRUITION

THOUGHT THIS WAS BLISS HEAVEN AT LAST

NOW IS THE FUTURE URGED BY THE PAST

BUT HEARTS CAN BE FRAGILE HARD TO RECOVER

FROM PROMISES BROKEN ADMITTING IT'S OVER

LOSING MOMENTUM A BRIEF HESISTATION

WHO WILL PAY DEARLY FOR RECRIMINATION

NO BLAME SHIFTING DON'T DESIGNATE

THE SILENCE OF EMPTINESS RESONATES

THE PASSING OF FLEETING JOY I WONDER

HOW IT TURNED IN A FLASH DRAGGING US UNDER

WAS IT UNREALISTIC TO CALL LOVE SO BRIEF

THAT IT ENDED ABRUPTLY IN SUCH PAINFUL GRIEF

48

WHAT TOOK YOU SO LONG TO GET HERE AT LAST

WITH THE WILDEST LOVE NO ONE HAD SURPASSED

WHAT TOOK YOU SO LONG TO JUST LET IT GO

WELL NEVER MIND IT WAS QUITE A SHOW

THE SUM OF NOTHING

ONE SIDED FRIENDSHIP IS WEARING THIN

LOST LOVE THROWN CARELESSLY TO THE WIND

THIS HEART'S BEATING FASTER JUST TO SURVIVE

PRAY DON'T BOTHER APOLOGIZE

TAKE ALL THAT WAS GOOD BEEN CAST AWAY

NOW LEFT WITH YESTERDAYS GIFT FOR A DAY

DISTURBING TO SENSE WHATS BECOME OF THE TIME

HOW LONG AGO'S PASSION SKIPPED A BEAT BEHIND

JUST A WEAK POSSIBILITY OF MEETING AGAIN

WITH LITTLE TO SAY SMILE OR CONTEND

NOT A HINT OF MEMORY TO PURSUE RUSHING

AGELESS AND TIMELESS THE SUM OF NOTHING

COVERED

WE WERE FLYING HIGH COVERED IN LOVE

CAUGHT IN AN AFTERNOON RAIN

WITH KISSES I COULDN'T GET ENOUGH OF

AND THINKING YOU FELT THE SAME

RUNNING THROUGH ASPEN COVERED IN SNOW

YOU CARRIED ME FOR A RUN

A THRILL RIDE LIKE I'VE NEVER KNOWN

JUST US TWO TUNE OUT EVERYONE

SUDDEN TOGETHERNESS COVERED THE LIVES

OF MORE THAN WHAT WE HAD STARTED

APPEALING NEW CLOSENESS WHAT DOES DRIVE

US TO SHOW OFF FEELINGS IMPARTED

MINE AND YOURS COVERED IN OURS

BROTHERS AND SISTERS TOGETHER

CLEARLY GROWTH AND TIME EMPOWERS

THEM WITH CONNECTION FOREVER

PHANTOM OF MINE COVERED IN MUSIC

THIS DREAM WASN'T MEANT TO BE

CONFUSION ABOUNDS HOW DID WE LOSE IT

FACED WITH THE COLD REALITY

OF TREACHEROUS LIES COVERED IN SMILES

THE PLAY YOU SKILLFULLY FASHIONED

FOOLED BY THE MASK BUT KNEW ALL THE WHILE

THE LACK OF TRUE LOVE'S PASSION

I WISH YOU

I WISH YOU WERE HONEST OPEN DIRECT

ANTICIPATED NOTHING LESS THAN PERFECT

I WISH YOU HAD SEEN SOMEONE ELSE BEYOND YOU

EMBRACING YOUR BEGUILING POINT OF VIEW

I WISH YOU A MIRROR TO SEE YOUR REFLECTION

THE GLASS TURNING CLOUDY WITH IMPERFECTIONS

I WISH YOU HAD FORESIGHT TO WHO MATTERED MOST

WHILE INFLICTING DISTRESS ON THOSE WHO WERE CLOSE

I WISH YOU THE POWER TO FINALLY SAY

THE WORDS I'M SORRY AND TO THIS VERY DAY

I WISH YOU HAD SAID THEM TIME AND AGAIN

TO KNOW THAT YOU COULD AND BE FORGIVEN

I WISH YOU INTEGRITY FOR FUTURE ENDEAVORS

TAKE IT TO HEART MAINTAIN IT FOREVER

ALL THIS WISHING IS FOOLISH WON'T DO ANY GOOD

IN THE END I WISH YOU MORE THAN I SHOULD

MY BEST FRIEND

IN THE BEGINNING WITH SO MUCH HOPE

MY FAITH IN WHAT I FEEL

GROWING STRONGER AND NOT A JOKE

WILL YOU AGREE TO MAKE IT REAL

OUR LIVES ALIGNED AS ONE IN TUNE

WITH PASSION MORE THAN THOUGHT

NO ROOM FOR DOUBT I FELT IMMUNE

TO PAIN CAUSED BY A BLIND SPOT

THE BUBBLE BURST MY DREAMS WERE LOST

UPON MY NEW DISCOVERY

YOU ALLOWED HER IN AT A GREATER COST

ADDING YEARS TO MY RECOVERY

YOUR PROMISE VANISHED ALL TOO SOON

WORDS LIKE GLASS THAT SHATTERED

OCCURRED TO ME THAT AFTERNOON

IT NEVER REALLY MATTERED

SO MUCH TIME HAS PASSED IN YEARS

NOT LOVE BUT IN THE END

LONG AGO I DRIED MY TEARS

YOU NEVER WERE MY BEST FRIEND

DANGEROUSLY CLOSE TO LOVE

DANGEROUSLY CLOSE TO LOVE

SOMETHING TO SPECULATE

OVER THE MOON AND ABOVE

LONGING TO ARTICULATE

BUT BEWARE EMOTIONS STRONG

CAREFUL FOR A MISSTEP

SIGNS COULD BE READ WRONG

ODDS WITH GUARD UP BEST

UNCERTAIN GLANCE OF PASSION

EXPRESSED WITH EYES AVERTED

A MOMENT WITHOUT ACTION

THRILL NOTED AS DESERTED

SET ASIDE FALSE PRETENCE

AMOROUS SOULS EXPOSED

CRUMBLED WALLS OF SELF-DEFENSE

IMPRESSIVE YET CONTROLLED

WITH PERSISTENT RESERVATION

CONFLICTING TRUTH OR LIES

NOT WITHOUT COMPLICATION

COMPREHEND OR COMPROMISE

CLOSE THE WOUND BEFORE IT BLEEDS

SHIELDED HEART BE TOUGH

FACED THE RISK RESOLVED THE NEED

DANGEROUSLY CLOSE TO LOVE

JUST WALK AWAY

WALK AWAY

LEAVE DON'T STAY

PROMISED YOU'D NEVER

TURN AWAY FROM ME EVER

WHO SAID I WOULD

FORGIVE YOU WHY SHOULD

I NOW THAT IT'S DONE

THE TRUTH IS I'VE WON

RUN WHAT'S THE MATTER

THE SOONER THE BETTER

I SAID IT GET OUT

I'M CALM BUT I'LL SHOUT

EQUIPPED WITH MY SADNESS

AND DEAL WITH THE MADNESS

OF GETTING YOU RID

FOR ALL THAT YOU DID

 GO AWAY SEARING PAIN

CAN'T YOU TAKE THE BLAME

WITH RESPONSIBILITY REALIZE

LET'S BE CLEAR DON'T PATRONIZE

ME WITH YOUR OH SO COOL

DEMEANOR I WON'T BE THE FOOL

WITHOUT MAKING A SOUND

STOP DON'T TURN AROUND

60

NOW HERE COMES GOODBYE

ODDS ARE I'LL CRY

AND WONDER QUITE POSSIBLY

WILL I SMILE AGAIN PROBABLY

IT'S RESOLVED I BELIEVE

WITH EMOTIONS RELIEVED

WHAT ELSE CAN I SAY

JUST WALK AWAY

THE WRONG FACE

I MIGHT HAVE BEEN MISTAKEN

THROUGH SHEETS OF POURING RAIN

INDEPENDENT OR FORSAKEN

RELIEF OR WASTED PAIN

AND EVEN AT A QUICK GLANCE

THE ANGLES NOT QUITE RIGHT

A MIRACLE OR ODDS BY CHANCE

ON A COLD AND BITTER NIGHT

SWIFTLY RUN FOR COVER

STOP MY HEART DON'T RACE

SAVE IT FOR ANOTHER

WITHOUT THREAT OF HEARTBREAK

PANIC WITH ANTICIPATION

AT BEST IMPROBABLE

HEATED ANGUISH AND FRUSTRATION

BREATHE AND LET IT GO

IN A MOMENT NOT OBSCURE

WITH SIGHTLINE CLEAR I COULD

DETECT HIS PRESENCE I WAS SURE

AND INDEED THERE HE STOOD

EMOTIONS HIGH OUT OF CONTROL

GAIN STRENGTH TO DISAPPEAR

FROM WILD DEMONS TAKING HOLD

MY CHEEKS STREAMING WITH TEARS

63

AS I STOOD THERE IN DISBELIEF

HIS APPEARANCE AT THIS PLACE

WAS APPARENTLY MISCONCEIVED

OF COURSE IT WAS THE WRONG FACE

LOOK FOR ME

LOOK FOR ME ON THE OTHER SIDE

DON'T KEEP ME WAITING LONG

CONFUSING THOUGH IT'S BEEN AT TIMES

WEAKENED HEARTS BE STRONG

LOOK FOR ME REACHING OUT

DRAW ME CLOSER IN

APART FROM YOU WITHOUT A DOUBT

THROW CAUTION TO THE WIND

LOOK FOR ME GLANCE BACK AND FIND

NO QUALMS OR PAUSE TO END

THE DREAM WHERE LOVE CAN'T BE DENIED

THAT DAY WE'LL BOTH TRANSCEND

THE GOOD NEWS IS

I'LL NEVER HAVE TO WONDER WHY

WON'T HAVE TO HEAR ANOTHER LIE

NO MORE NEED TO HAVE YOUR BACK

ENDURE MALEVOLENT ATTACKS

NOT LISTEN TO THE BOASTFUL BANTER

REPLYING TO IT DOESN'T MATTER

NO MORE WORRY FOR WELL BEING

AND ALL ELSE NOW CLEARLY SEEING

HOW YOU USED THAT FALSE BRAVADO

SHRINKING BACK INTO SHADOWS

GIVING THOSE AROUND YOU BLAME

WHILE YOU COLLECTED ALL THE FAME

HEARTACHE'S SONG ALLEVIATED

UNTOUCHED RESOLVE BECAME OUTDATED

GOODBYES OMITTED WITHOUT SORROW

THE BEST FOR LAST WITHOUT TOMORROW

WAS THIS A LIFETIME OF DENIAL

DEATH HAS A WAY TO MAKE IT FINAL

AUTISM LIVES HERE...

"IF I CAN'T TELL YOU EXACTLY HOW I FEEL

OR ACT OUT IN A WAY THAT SEEMS UNREAL

YOU'RE EVERYTHING I COUNT ON EVERY DAY

DO ACCEPT ME AND CHERISH MY OWN SPECIAL WAY"

I AM SPECIAL JUST LIKE YOU

I AM SPECIAL JUST LIKE YOU

I CAN TAKE THE THINGS I DO

AND LEARN FROM THEM THE BEST I CAN

MAKE A DIFFERENCE WITH WHO I AM

YOU MIGHT BE SLOW AND I MIGHT BE FAST

WE DON'T NEED TO MEASURE WHO IS FIRST OR LAST

YOU MIGHT BE SMART AND I MAY BE NOT

SO WHO CARES ABOUT THAT WE STILL HAVE A LOT

TO SHARE AND TO GROW TOGETHER WE'LL BE

FRIENDS TO THE END JUST YOU WAIT AND SEE

I KEEP TO MYSELF QUIET AS A MOUSE

QUIET IS GOOD IN THIS VERY BIG HOUSE

THE NOISE THE NOISE THAT GETS TOO LOUD

IF WE'RE SHOPPING OR IN A BIG CROWD

IT CAN COME FROM THE TV OR RADIO MUSIC

WHATEVER IT IS I CAN EASILY LOSE IT

IT BOTHERS ME EVERYWHERE AND STARTS TO HURT

IN MY EARS AND MY HEAD AND I'M JUST NOT SURE

HOW TO STOP IT BUT WISH I COULD FIGURE IT OUT

WHAT IS THIS TERRIBLE NOISE ALL ABOUT

I AM A HAPPY KID MOST OF THE TIME

AND SMILE AT EVERYONE I CAN FIND

IF I DON'T UNDERSTAND I EASILY CRY

WISH I COULD TELL YOU I JUST DON'T KNOW WHY

SOMETIMES WHEN YOU SPEAK

I'M NOT SURE WHAT YOU SAY

IF YOU'RE SAD OR YOU'RE HURT

I MIGHT NOT HEAR IT THAT WAY

I LIKE IT WHEN THINGS ARE ALWAYS THE SAME

LIKE MY FOOD AND TOYS AND MY VIDEO GAMES

I WALK ON MY TOES AND TWIRL ROUND AND ROUND

IT MAKES ME FEEL BETTER AND HELPS ME CALM DOWN

LISTENING TO SOUNDS THAT YOU DON'T WANT TO HEAR

TAKE YOUR OWN HANDS AND COVER YOUR EARS

IF I WERE A TURTLE I COULD MOVE MY HEAD FAST

BACK INTO MY SHELL WHERE IT'S QUIET AT LAST

SOMETIMES WHEN WE TALK I DON'T LOOK IN YOUR EYES

I MIGHT JUST FORGET SO DON'T BE SURPRISED

IF I DON'T SPEAK AT ALL LET'S TRY TO WAIT

THERE ARE OTHER WAYS WE CAN COMMUNICATE

IT'S HARD TO SIT STILL WHEN I WANT TO PLAY

I START MOVING AROUND IN MY OWN SPECIAL WAY

WHEN I GET EXCITED I CAN KEEP MYSELF BUSY

BY JUMPING AND SPINNING EVEN THOUGH I GET DIZZY

I CAN PLAY WITH MY HANDS AND FINGERS ALL OVER

IT'S JUST WHAT I DO NO NEED TO TAKE COVER

WHEN I'M FINALLY TIRED I DO REALIZE

IT'S THE END OF TODAY AND CAN JUST CLOSE MY EYES

THINGS DON'T LOOK THE SAME TO YOU AND ME

WHERE I SEE A FOREST YOU SEE A TREE

I HEAR THE WIND BLOWING STRONG IN THE SKY

YOU HEAR A BREEZE AS IT SOFTLY GOES BY

MY SMELL AND MY TASTE ARE DIFFERENT THAN YOURS

SO MANY CHOICES THANK GOODNESS OF COURSE

THERE'S REALLY A LOT TO SAY ABOUT TOUCH

SOMETIMES EVEN MY CLOTHES FEEL TOO MUCH

IF I THINK THE LIGHT IS SHINING TOO BRIGHT

OR EVEN IF THE NOISE ISN'T RIGHT

IF IT SMELLS AWFUL AND TASTES BAD

AND ANYTHING TOUCHING MAKES ME MAD

IT'S A TERRIBLE TIME FOR YOU AND ME

BUT IT PASSES SO QUICKLY AND SOON WE WILL SEE

THAT IT'S OVER AND DONE WITH AND BETTER AT LAST

IT WAS JUST A QUICK MOMENT NOW GONE IN THE PAST

SAY WHAT YOU SAY EASY AND CLEAR

I ONLY UNDERSTAND EXACTLY WHAT I HEAR

IF I CAN'T FIND THE RIGHT WORDS TO ANSWER YOU

WATCH ME CAREFULLY LOOK AT WHAT I DO

WHEN ALL THOSE WORDS GET IN THE WAY

I LEARN BEST WHEN I SEE IT EVERY DAY

BE PATIENT WITH ME IT DOES TAKE ME TIME

LET'S SAY IT AND DO IT 'TIL MY MIND

CAN FIGURE IT OUT SO I CAN TELL

WHAT I NEEDED AND REMEMBER IT WELL

AS I GROW BIGGER AND STRONGER EACH DAY

I HOPE I CAN FIND AN EASIER WAY

TO SAY WHAT I THINK AND THINK WHAT I FEEL

HOW GREAT THAT WOULD BE A REALLY BIG DEAL

I CAN DO BETTER WHEN YOU THINK THAT I CAN

REMEMBER TO SHOW ME AND SHOW ME AGAIN

I KNOW THAT YOU LOVE ME SO LOVE ME THROUGH THIS

I DO MY BEST AND DON'T NEED TO BE FIXED

HELP ME AND TEACH ME IT'S SIMPLE AS THAT

I NEED YOU I LOVE YOU MATTER OF FACT

74

IF I CAN'T TELL YOU EXACTLY HOW I FEEL

OR ACT OUT IN A WAY THAT SEEMS UNREAL

YOU'RE EVERYTHING I COUNT ON EVERY DAY

DO ACCEPT ME AND CHERISH MY OWN SPECIAL WAY

AUTISM LIVES HERE

AUTISM LIVES HERE YES IT DOES

WITHOUT WARNING OR PLAN

EXPLAIN THE REASON CLEARLY BECAUSE

WE NEED TO UNDERSTAND

THE WHY AND THE WHEREFORE

THE CAUSE AND THE FIX

GIVE DETAILS AND THEN MORE

WITHOUT THE CONFLICTS

WHAT MORE CAN WE POSSIBLY DO

TO OFFER COMFORT AND EASE

COULD THERE BE A MIRACLE BREAKTHROUGH

AND BY THE WAY PLEASE

DON'T JUDGE SO QUICKLY NEXT TIME

YOU ENCOUNTER AN INTERACTION

THAT COULD BE CONSTRUED AS WILD

BUT DESERVING REAL COMPASSION

AUTISM LIVES HERE YES IT DOES

IT'S SPREAD WIDELY AMONG

A NEW GENERATION OF KIDS WITH LOVE

SOMEWHAT FRAGILE AND YOUNG

TO DEVELOP WITHIN THEIR CONDITION

WHILE LEARNING TO CONTROL

WHAT HOPEFULLY COMES TO FRUITION

TO REACH THEIR ULTIMATE GOAL

CAN WE DISTINGUISH THE DIFFERENCE

CAUGHT IN CONFUSION OR

BEHAVIOR CREATING INFERENCE

OF UNRULY CHAOTIC UPROAR

SO HERE'S TO APPRECIATION

OF PARENTS THAT HOLD STRONG

AND PRAISE THEIR DEDICATION

AND KNOW THEY'RE NOT ALONE

THE BEST PART OF ME

THE PART OF ME

THAT GET'S STUCK IN MY MIND

IS ALWAYS THERE HIDING

I'M WAITING TO FIND

THE WAY OUT TO EXPLAIN

WHAT I'M TRYING TO SAY

TO MAKE SURE IT'S NOT JUMBLED

AND COMES OUT THE RIGHT WAY

THE PART OF ME

LIKE TESTING NEW FOOD

WHEN MY TASTERS ARE READY

TO GET IN THE MOOD

FOR ONE BITE THAT'S PLENTY

IF IT'S NOT QUITE RIGHT NOW

NEXT TIME IT'S DELICIOUS

AND DESERVING A WOW

THE PART OF ME

THAT MAKES ME WONDER

WILL I THINK CLEARLY

AND PULL IT FROM UNDER

THE COVERS OF MY MIND

TO HELP ME EXPLORE

YES I KNOW I WILL FIND

HOW TO UNDERSTAND MORE

THE BEST PART OF ME

IS YET TO ARRIVE

PUT THE PUZZLE TOGETHER

MAKE MY REALITY THRIVE

80

AND ONE DAY WILL BECOME

WHAT I HOPE IT WILL BE

MY GROWN UP VERSION

THE BEST PART OF ME

AND THEN THERE'S ALWAYS ...
DREAMS AND DEATH

"SHE LEANED OVER AND TOUCHED ME OF THIS I AM SURE

HER HAND ON MINE BUT IT WAS JUST THE ALLURE

OF RECAPTURING LIFE AND HAVING HER NEAR

FOR THE BRIEFEST OF MOMENTS TO REAPPEAR"

HAVE YOU GONE AWAY

HAVE YOU GONE AWAY

I NEVER WILL FORGET

WAS IT JUST YESTERDAY

OR SOONER EVEN YET

THAT YOU CLOSED YOUR EYES

AND GAVE YOUR HAND TO ME

COMFORT AND A WARM SURPRISE

JUST THOUGHT YOU'D ALWAYS BE

DOWN THE BLOCK AROUND THE CORNER

SOMEWHERE WITHIN MY SIGHT

FOREVER FEELING LIKE A MOURNER

HAVE WE LOST THIS FIGHT

HAVE YOU GONE AWAY

I CAN'T BELIEVE IT'S TRUE

I KNOW YOU'RE STILL HERE STAY

WE'VE SO MUCH MORE TO DO

I'M LIFTED WHEN YOU'RE NEAR

VALUE YOUR OPINION

OF COURSE IT'S CRYSTAL CLEAR

TOGETHER WE'RE A GIVEN

WON'T BETRAY YOUR TRUST

I'LL KEEP THE SECRET CLOSE

PAINFUL MISS YOU MUCH

AND NOW I NEED TO KNOW

HAVE YOU GONE AWAY

I'M THANKFUL JUST TO SHARE

IMAGINARY TIME TODAY

OUR CONNECTION IS STILL THERE

I SPEAK TO YOU OUT LOUD

WAITING FOR THE ANSWER

YOU GIVE WITHOUT A SOUND

RESPONSES THAT I TREASURE

DO WE HAVE TO PART

PROMISE THAT YOU'LL STAY

I BEG DON'T BREAK MY HEART

HAVE YOU GONE AWAY

HEAVEN IN DREAMS

AN INTRODUCTION TO SELF EXPRESSION

MY FIRST AND UNUSUAL DREAM OF HEAVEN

ARRIVING NOT A MOMENT TOO SOON

TO THE DELICATE FRAGRANCE OF FLOWERS IN BLOOM

I WANDERED AROUND THROUGH THE TRANQUIL AIR

WHILE THEY WATCHED ME IN WONDER WITHOUT A CARE

THERE THEY STOOD EVERYONE GATHERED

BEAUTIFUL CREATURES OF EVERY STATURE

THE REMARKABLE THING AND BEST OF ALL

I CAUGHT A GLIMPSE OF AUNT SONJA GRAND AND TALL

I KNEW SHE HAD PASSED A SHORT TIME BEFORE

SO SMALL AND FRAGILE NOW ROBUST AND MORE

LARGER THAN LIFE AND COULD IT POSSIBLY BE

THAT AUNT SONJA WAS GOD AND HE WAS A SHE

WITH GOLDEN RED HAIR CURLED ROUND HER HEAD

FROM HER BLUE GINGHAM APRON SHE EAGERLY SPREAD

A RAINBOW OF MORSELS UPON THE SUNLIT FLOOR

TO FEED ALL THE PRIVILEGED THAT SHE CARED FOR

I SUDDENLY REALIZED THAT I WAS THE ONLY

PERSON IN HEAVEN AND TURNED AROUND SLOWLY

THE VISION WAS BREATHTAKING SERENE WITH PEACE

AS HARMONY FILTERED THROUGHOUT THE SPACE

HEAVEN WAS TRULY A JUBILANT PLACE

EVERYONE BUSY AND I SAW BY HER FACE

NOW WAS THE TIME TO COME BACK FROM MY DREAM

AND REMEMBER FOR YEARS THAT BEAUTIFUL SCENE

MOTHER IN DREAMS

IN DREAMS SHE WAS LAUGHING AS MOTHERS DO

HOW LUCKY I AM TO HAVE A GIRL LIKE YOU

YOU ARE THE MAGIC AND WILL ALWAYS BE

BEAUTIFUL THE SMARTEST THE BEST TO ME

HER VISITS A THRILL THOUGH SOMETIMES CONFUSING

REMINISCING THE PAST AND MUCH AMUSING

ENRICHING MY LIFE WE HAVE ALWAYS BEEN

THE BEST OF FRIENDS CLOSER THAN SKIN

SHE LEANED OVER AND TOUCHED ME OF THIS I AM SURE

HER HAND ON MINE BUT IT WAS JUST THE ALLURE

OF RECAPTURING LIFE AND HAVING HER NEAR

FOR THE BRIEFEST OF MOMENTS TO REAPPEAR

88

LINGERING JOY NO THOUGHT TO FORSAKE

UNTIL I MADE THE ULTIMATE MISTAKE

OF SOBBING IN SLEEP WITH TEARS I COULD FEEL

SHE MUST STILL BE WITH ME IN DREAMS IT WAS REAL

FEAR IN DREAMS

IN DREAMS OF MY NANA DOWN BY THE OCEAN

FROM A SMALL WINDOW THE SHADOW IN MOTION

LURKED IN A DARKNESS I COULDN'T QUITE SEE

WHILE SHE TURNED BACK AND SMILED AT ME

UNAWARE OF THE DANGER SHE STOPPED TO WAVE

THROUGH ENDLESS SAND SHE CONTINUED TO PAVE

HER WAY TOWARD THE WATER WITHOUT FEAR

AS HE ALMOST REACHED HER A DISTANCE TOO NEAR

I NEEDED TO WARN HER AND WHIRLED AROUND

SHOUTING OUT LOUD BUT NOT MAKING A SOUND

I TOOK A DEEP BREATH AND TRIED IT AGAIN

TO NO AVAIL I PANICKED AND THEN

90

HE WAS GONE IN A FLASH TEARS WELLED IN MY EYES

FEAR AND FRUSTRATION AGONIZE

A SIGH OF RELIEF FOR THE MOMENT HAD PASSED

DREAMS THAT ARE NIGHTMARES HOW LONG WILL IT LAST

WAITING

WALKING THROUGH LIFE NOW BLACK AND WHITE

THE COLORS OF DAY FADE TO DISMAL NIGHT

WEEKS TURNED TO MONTHS AND QUICKLY TO YEARS

TIME SPEEDING BY AND NOW FILLED WITH FEARS

DAYDREAMED AND WISHED FOR ONCE UPON A TIME

IMPATIENCE THE WEAKNESS ALWAYS THE CRIME

NEVER STOOD STILL LONG ENOUGH TO ENJOY

THE BEST OF MOMENTS LEFT TO DESTROY

RANDOM DOORS OPENED AND LITTLE SUCCESS

FROM CHALLENGE TO EFFORT TO FAILURE AND STRESS

THINK OF IDEAS CREATE ONE IN KIND

FRANTICALLY SEARCHING FOR ONE I MIGHT FIND

92

BUT PROSPECTS ARE FEW NONEXISTENT AND COLD

HOW DID I PICTURE MYSELF GROWING OLD

ADMITTING THAT THERE'S NO THE PIE IN THE SKY

ALL THAT IS LEFT IS JUST WAITING TO DIE

FLYING IN DREAMS

IN DREAMS OF UNKNOWN AND WHO KNOWS WHY

I WAS LOST IN THE AIR ATTEMPTING TO FLY

I STEPPED OFF A LANDING AND FELT STRANGELY FREE

AS I LOOKED DOWN THERE'S NO NET TO CATCH ME

NOTHING ALARMING I COULD SOAR TO NEW HEIGHTS

THERE I FLOATED WITH EASE AMONG STARRY LIGHTS

BUT WHY I WAS FLYING DIDN'T MAKE ANY SENSE

I SUDDENLY REALIZED I WAS TERRIBLY TENSE

IN PANIC I REACHED FOR WHATEVER I COULD

BUT NOTHING OF SAFETY TO GRASP THAT WOULD

SAVE ME FROM FALLING AT A STARTLING RATE

IN DREAMS AND UNEXPECTEDLY I WAS AWAKE

DEATH IN DREAMS

IN DREAMS MINE DO LEAN TOWARD THE BIZARRE

PLAYING MY EMOTIONS TEARING THROUGH MY HEART

REALISTIC OFTEN FRIGHTENING AS THOUGH I WERE THERE

IN THE DARKNESS ALONE AND UNABLE TO BEAR

DESPERATELY PRAYING THIS COULDN'T BE DEATH

TO ONE I LOVE MOST NOT TAKING A BREATH

CRUMPLED UP LAYING A CHILD OF MINE

AS DISBELIEF AND HORROR COMBINE

OH NO PLEASE GOD DON'T LET IT BE

YOU'D BE MUCH BETTER OFF TAKING ME

THERE'S A FUTURE CREATING STILL YEARS AWAY

FOR THIS BEAUTIFUL CHILD YOU MUST LET STAY

SUDDENLY SOBBING CONFUSED AND AWAKE

JUST A HORRIBLE NIGHTMARE FILLED WITH HEARTBREAK

RELIEVED THE NEXT DAY I HELD ON TOO TIGHT

NEVER COULD SAY WHAT WAS IN DREAMS THAT NIGHT

AFTER LIFE

IT WASN'T LIKE HEAVEN OF THIS I WAS SURE

AN UNFAMILIAR PLACE RATHER OBSCURE

POTENTIALLY FLOATING OR BEING UPLIFTED

FREE FROM POSSESSION AND YET RESTRICTED

NOT HOT AS HELL OR COLD AS THE FREEZER

BUT SOMEWHERE BETWEEN PAIN AND PLEASURE

BARELY A SOUND AND VOID OF EMOTION

NO SAND OF THE DESERT OR MIST FROM THE OCEAN

NOT ESPECIALLY CLEAN OR DIRT ANYWHERE

BUT WELL ORGANZIED TAKEN WITH CARE

97

NOT AN ENEMY IN SIGHT NEITHER A FRIEND

NOBODY TO LEAN ON HOLD OR DEPEND

USE ALL RESOURCEFULNESS MAKE A PLAN

A LONG WAIT AHEAD THAT COULD POSSIBLY SPAN

FIVE OR TEN OR ONE MILLION YEARS

WITHOUT FRUSTRATION OR NEED FOR TEARS

ALMOST AN OUT OF BODY EXPERIENCE

OF ONE WHO IS CAUGHT IN WAVES OF DELIRIOUS

THOUGHTS CAN I MAKE AN APPEAL FOR A POSSIBLE

CHANGE OF SCENARY TO MAKE IT MORE PLAUSIBLE

www.ingramcontent.com/pod-product-compliance
Lightning Source LLC
Chambersburg PA
CBHW031315060726

47590CB00003B/1218